THE LIGHT WILL ALWAYS RETURN

Poems

Frank McMahon

Tim Saunders Publications

Cover design: Miserden Lake, Gloucestershire,
a photograph by Frank McMahon

This book is dedicated to:

Dorothy
Anna and Jonathan
Mark and Ione
Sam, Tom and Dora
Orla, Briony and Aggie.

Light and *shadow* are both basic descriptions of physical phenomena and widely used as metaphors. These images/metaphors have for me a timeless resonance and they influenced my choice of title for this, my third collection of poems. To give just one example which inspired me, "I must know my shadow and my light" are some of the closing lines from Sir Michael Tippett's Oratorio, "A Child of our Time"; lines in which he prompts us to move away from hatred towards the 'better angels' of our nature. (His work was written in response to events in Nazi Germany.)

The theme of *light* recurs throughout the whole volume, beginning directly with the first section, Prelude. *Shadow* and *darkness* appear in varied guises: grief, war, social distress. The 8th century Chinese poet, Du Fu, wrote, "joy and sadness take turns in a dance beyond our control." This is the world we inhabit and my feelings about that surface in some of the poems.

I have also tried to create a stage for those un-named craftsmen/women and artists whose beautiful creations illuminate our world.

Finally, some of the poems arise from those wonderful experiences which just stopped me in my tracks where I forgot everything else.

Thank you for choosing to read these poems. I hope they entertain, stimulate, engage you and strike a deeper chord.

If you would like to share your reactions I would love to hear them. I can be reached through Facebook or Twitter, FrankMcMah56434.

Frank McMahon
Cirencester 2024

BIOGRAPHICAL NOTE

I live in Cirencester, am married with two children and six grandchildren. My professional career was in Social Work/Welfare.

I have two books of poems: At The Storm's Edge and A Different Land, published by Palewell Press, the second published in 2022. I have won the Gloucestershire Writers Network first prize for poetry. I have also been published in Acumen and have had more work accepted by Indigo Dreams.

Previous work has appeared in The Cannon's Mouth, Riggwelter, Morphrog, Brittlestar, The Curlew, Makarelle, Writeresque, Erbacce, I am not a Silent Poet, Fly on the Wall and Voices for the Silent.

In 2021 and 2023, I read at Cheltenham Poetry Festival ann Cheltenham Literary Festival in 2022 and 2023.

PRELUDE

AS THE EARTH TILTS

Angled light, spear-tipped,
jabs at retina, induces
tears of premature surrender.

Wind disperses mist
like a cataract excised;
every twig of oak revealed
by the pouring light.

Winter light, when you stand
concealed from the northern wind,
wraps itself around like a woollen shawl.

Dawn's thin emerging stripe
promises tangerine, persimmon,
deeper blue than forget-me-not,
rainbows in a field of frost.

Crystal winter light
a vessel to hold and savour
Atlantic salt, smoky peat and iodine,
summers' heat upon your tongue.

From under rocks and tombstones
strangled light emerges, ashen;
the soul groans, gives way.

The gift of rationed daylight doubles itself,
is cherished for its chords of hope,
its heart of memory and promise.

Lux aeterna.
Imagine the time before the stars,
dark void churning.

Es war licht!

Feux grisâtres, feux éclatants,
n'importe quoi, bienvenus!

Winter starlight
inverted bowl of silver grapes,
distant flicker of succulence.

WATER MUSIC

RIVER SONG

The held note of this river
cannot be heard unless you kneel
upon the bank, lower your head to within
a finger's length; and wait.

The held note of this river may be
the pause between the breaths
of an infant in sleep profound
a bow poised above strings
vibration of a spider's web
heads bowed towards the catafalque.

The held note of this river
is molecular, contained
until it knows you give attention,
concentrate as if a tongue-tied child strives to bring
the painful weight of words to lips.

The held note of this river
carries a message which only you
can write and then and only then
will it release its music.

WHO OWNS A RIVER?

Pretentious claims
of fences, fences, fences,
water bailiffs, warning signs.

Trout, mayfly, dipper
crowsfoot and kingcups
inscribe their precious byelaws;
graffiti falls from anarchic clouds.

Water has no title deeds,
runs defenceless.

The dipped hand in this river,
here before word and name,
here, then and now.

EMPEROR AKHBAR SEEKS ULTIMATE TRUTH

In the red sandstone tower he takes his seat,
greets again the priests of different faiths.
For months
he's taken time away from the chores of ruling,
time to explore which faith has the lock on truth.
He's heard their claims, unwavering assertions.

This morning he's come with a novel question.
"Where does a river start?"

Where it bubbles from a spring.
No, from the aquifer below.
No, from the rains which fell.
No, from the clouds which brought the rain.
No, from the winds which brought the clouds.
No, from the vapour lifting from the sea.
No, from the river which feeds the sea.

He rises. "Send me a message when you have all
agreed."
He descends and walks towards his palace, knowing
it was wrong to build it here,
this site of desert winds and failing streams.

FOWEY

"Saint James, grant us safe passage to your shrine.
Our eyes know land and our feet
the sturdiness of soil and rock. Salt-fish, yes
but not their home, not tide nor swell nor breakers,
wooden walls or flapping sails. Guide us over
the trackless waters while we pray against tempests.
How many days till we come to you not even those
who take us there can say. Lord, as the rope
is loosened from the ring, bind us closer to your
mercy."

An army gathers, hunkered in steel against
the blasting gale and rain; arms and ordnance,
flesh and fear, last letters home. (How many will give
the last full measure of devotion?)
Night falls: a signal flares from St Katherine's Hill.
The hawsers coiled, anchors weighed, conjoined
the pulse of hearts and engines. The river
has done its duty, midwife to destruction.

The banks are set with oaks, like broccoli on display.
The river narrows, its harbour absorbs trawlers,
yachts and smacks, safe home
in the westward-falling light.

CRAFTWORK

SAVING BYZANTIUM

Every time he asks
is this allowed?
They do not paint God's face,
our enemies. They are
ocean, plague, unanswered swords,
surely God must love them more?

They tell him: this is a settled question
and this is your commission,
The Triumph of Orthodoxy.
Only God and Faith can save this city now.
So pray, forgive your enemies,
paint as if God is with you in this room.

The monk takes wood and tempera
creates within the icon
a copy of a second, ancient and revered.
Hodegetria. Child and Virgin veiled in damson blue,
the frame red like ripening mulberry,
held by saints against a wall of gold.
Martyrs, Emperor and Patriarch,
Byzantium summoning the past
to stand against the future.

Historical note:

The Triumph of Orthodoxy is an icon created in Constantinople around 1370 CE when the Byzantine Empire was under mortal threat from Turkish, Islamic armies.

The Empire stood alone and the icon was created to show the people what the Empire would look like when God protected it.

It is based on a much earlier icon, Hodgeteria, created in 843 on the orders of Empress Theodosia to show that it was permissible to have images which showed the godhead.

There had been major disputes as to whether this was acceptable.

More information can be found in The History of the World in 100 objects by Neil MacGregor (2010) and by looking online for pictures of both icons.

THE BROKEN COLUMN
(After Frida Kahlo)

If I must be bound by the surgeon's hoops and skills
if I must be bound to repair this wounded flesh
if I must be bound so that
bone will bind and lock me from within
though I must be bound
I will succumb only to ambition.

Though I must lie prone
I will walk in my galleries of time,
though I must lie within white sheets
their threads will weave for me
every new green spring and the irrepressible sea;
though I must be bound you will find me in the desert,
a pillar of restless, lacerated fire.

MOSAIC

1

I held my breath as she braced
the tiny stone on a block of wood
between two long and supple fingers,
lifted the heavy hammer-axe
on a perfect arc
and brought it down,
one exactly angled blow
to smooth the ruckled surface.

2

Eagle-beaked, twin-headed hammer,
razor-edged,
tempered steel on a hardwood haft
rests on a trunk of oak in the pupils' room;
it would look more at home in a climber's hand
scaling a wall of ice than here,
where a scatter of stone and rock waits
to be shaped to fit mosaic patterns.

3

Practice, practice, practice
to master the precision
of angled strikes
where one false stroke
could sever finger-tips.

4

Learn the qualities of stones,
texture, potential
for longevity;
immerse yourself in colours,
blend art and craft and teamwork.

5

A rainbow waterfall
spills downwards
and floods across the floor;
"Guernica" hangs on an outside wall.

6

Cross-legged in the ancient church
she sifts for shape and palette
tests for the millimetric fit,
sets tesserae in a bed of stucco;
hour after hour until the old saint
can rest, restored,
faith and mastery combined.

SOURDOUGH

Does it have to be like this? My hands trapped
in this ectoplasmic blob. It seemed harmless
last night when I laid it down to rise.
I really should have picked a simpler task:
making sense of quantum physics, riding
a penny-farthing in a force nine gale.

No use now as I wrestle with this dough,
nay, monster. First proving, I slathered you
in olive oil. Was I too rough as I
pounded and pummelled, stretched, stretched,
stretched you out,
a line of white intestine? Entrapment
was your game, yet I have tamed you with my
farinaceous hands, caressed and then reformed
you, laid you in the tin, a baby in its cradle.

Say not that the struggle naught availeth
as the firm, warm bread nestles in my palms.

GLASS

1

Me, me, me! My call,
that's all you'll know of me,
for you won't ever see
the bird who's made of glass. I'm faster
than the falcon when it stoops, more cunning
than the cuckoo, an avian chameleon.
I was born of alchemy, to perch in the Pharaoh's palace,
be admired and gather dust. But my mother
was too clever, gave me flight and changing colour.
I was off!
I've watched our spreading kingdom.
Tireless and garrulous,
ubiquitous historian.
Me! Me! Me!

2

They have many voices but in plain sight
have hidden their tongues. Until today.
Now I bid them speak, reveal themselves.

3

"Most loved, most hated, I show
only what is shown.
I map histories in sighs and wrinkles.
Most loved, most hated,
never easy speaking truth to power."

4

"Phials, test tubes, windows and syringes,
carboys, bottles, magnums and Methuselahs,
glass eyes and retorts.
Stop, stop, you've made your point!
No, no, not yet! Just one more.
No pane, no gain!"

5

"Heat, ah heat. I am being purified,
readied to receive. Then strips of orange
swim inside the hot and tawny mix
filling my capacious emptiness, jostle
and settle as heat falls upwards.
Sealed in silence, I embrace, preserve,
my role to await another's pleasure."

6

"Where, where, where am i, am i,
am i, where am i, where?
How can i retract my splintered shards
from these bodies, from this blood,
retract and reassemble unblemished?"

7

"It was that moment, dizzied by spinning,
molten and aloft, feeling a cooler, momentary
breath, then the shock of icy water,
it was that moment when I sensed
a shape, a becoming. What I was before
I do not know. I saw my sisters forming
and how they came to that is mystery.
It did not hurt when I was cut,
whorls and spirals emerging like blossoms
out of snow. Now we are held, filled
with a chilled liquid, warmed by lips of rose."

8

"Think or call me brash when I assert
that I bring to them the moving pictures
of the world beyond. Both the fixed:
walls, pylons, chimneys, solar panels.
And people passing by, I bring to them you,
in shirt or dress or sari; or child
with runny nose pressed against what was once
immaculate! In my largesse, I can forgive
this runty him or her for I am
indispensable, translucent Janus, bowing
inwards to keep the winds at bay on your behalf.
Respect me, nurture me. I am not like that thrush,
able to oil its plumage. So preen me. Preeeeen.
And yes, when it grows dark, it is acceptable
to draw the curtains, close the blinds.
Eyes require rest and the mind time
to plan the next day's show."

9

"When low, grey cloud scrapes
against the walls, spits
motes and dirt upon my ancient face,
I search for the yellow glow
of candles in the shadowed nave.
I am the faded rose,
etiolated sky,
curled husk of citrus,
holding to hope even from declining light."

10

"Ground to perfection, silent through upsurge
and vibration, silent through dark.
A sense of growing detachment.
Glass must be patient. And patient.

"Now I am released to scan the skies:
moons, clouds of gas, red and orange flares
erupting soundlessly, nebulae and star bursts.
Steered through ancestral dust,
I peer, I take, I send the sights
of the moving horizon. Where I began."

TUNNELLING WAVES
(after Barbara Hepworth's "Wave")

I must be engulfed between the arching lips
of this endless, breaking wave. I must churn
over and over within shoal-chants,
rhythmic thud of flukes, shingle-shift, chase
the promise or illusion of something beyond
tentative,
juggle word and sound along this abacus of tensile
strings,
which hold apart the waves' entombment. I must
play,
arrange again, again until the song sings itself
ashore,

where it must learn to walk and fly
before the tide re-asserts its claim.

IN MEMORIAM

HERE IS A PHOTOGRAPH
(i.m.Dora)

I did not take of you.

Strong pliable fingers, hours of interweaving
pliant strands of wicker
to build this vessel. Try to find
a beginning or an end
in the cross-hatched seams
which swayed once and greened,
filleted the sun
and shrouded warblers' nests.

Here is a photograph I could not take
of you
and if I had
impossible to share it now:
a Moses basket
absolute silence
save for the heart beating with grief,
a camera lens a sacrilege.

You're always here, engraved.

THE SIGNS OF THE CROSS

Rural certainties; the farm at the end
of the old boreen, sibling noise and play,
plod of cattle to the milking shed.
A neighbourhood of rules and obligations, pleasures
taken but never to excess.

Fresh eggs daily,
fish caught in buckets from the river;
around the kitchen table talk of weather
(rain was always guaranteed),
pests on the fruit, daily chores assigned,
news from the Great War somewhere over there.

Evening prayers, the immutable authority
of custom, church and school,
the maps of faith etched daily line by line.

Low voices carried upstairs: Black and Tans,
so and so killed, houses burned out. How safe
when a lorry might arrive, arrogant and lawless
or men might emerge from a hedgerow,
wave guns, usher you past?

The child begins to learn how to weigh words
against tone of voice, and eyes which flicker like a
bird flying sideways.

Sundays, the churchyard terse with a litany
of whispers, hooded looks.
Back home, father off-guard,
"Thank God for all our daughters
and our only son a boy. We farm and pray,
that's all we've ever done."

One by one, the family dissolves
to other lands and distant cities.

The grown child follows the road
to the station and the rough sea voyage,
faith her staff and guide
through romance, family, war and death,
through and beyond the fatal diagnosis.

CALL OF DUTY

Who would see that crossing as exotic?
Swift, oil-glossed currents of the Mersey,
war-maimed wharves, windows bleared with grime, empty
shattered ground, determined scrub. Exotic?
More used to games in cobbled entries, us brothers did,
chafing for the ferry, to race upstairs,
take up our station in the prow, vibrate
to the deepening thrum of engines
towards the Liver Buildings,
clang of trams, hustle of thicker accents.
What was not exotic?

Seaworthy. To make sure the ship is.
Will be through every turbulent ocean,
safe from human error.
I understand it better now, his work, something like,
"will this child be safe at home?"
Full circle of experience, he'd witnessed men killed
at sea.

This was our father's daily journey, nothing exotic.
Other words are needed: dutiful, conscientious,
impelled.

VOICES

They emerged and sang
"Requiem Aeternam,"
with the ache of a cauterised wound;
point and counterpoint rebounded
off fractured walls
as they probed into what remained unvoiced,
the mysterious gaps between the notes,
tasting their vinegar and honey.

I saw them leave homewards
to hunt for food and water
repair newly-opened scars
salvage hope from the wreckage of jagged days,

until they could recall their passion, their inner
voice,
find a yard of sun,
gather again along the line of song

"luft"   lift   lifting.
Voices   Voices   Voices
blending, moving through shattered windows.
And people came, curious,
drawn to the urgent sounds,
"Pacem, pacem, dona nobis pacem."
A siren groaned, a child looked skywards.

Voices, louder,
caressing every note,
in unison, unyielding.

THE JOURNEY NEVER TAKEN
(i.m Dora)

In Borrowdale
we stand high above the valley
which you will never see.
Imagine

a gallery of time and we were birds in flight
above a river of burnished ice,
year-on-year returning to view its diminution,
and catalogue what followed: seed drop,
slow spread of iridescent green, forest,
spaces to create a home,
endure, enjoy the seasons' circulations.
Now

we must imagine tracking our human selves,
footsore, descending the marked and ancient path,
all five senses open, filling like sails before the wind,
open,
for the spirits of this place must travel through us,
into bones, veins, membranes, cells
if we hope to carry with us all that we can never take
away:
rush of water down Stonethwaite Beck,
swallows' chase and meadowsweet's dance.
That should have been the start of exploration
of fractals and infinities. After, we could have said

at least we made a start, begun our precious archive.
That journal now fills with empty pages.

So, being bird, I have built for you a nest
gathered from what was gained
and what was lost.

OPENING OUT

HEDGEROWS

Autumn hedgerows after rain.
Ivy, sycamore and blackthorn profuse,
beaded with silver, rouge cascading ribbons
of rosehip and hawthorn berries;
and dusky sloes dreamy as lover's eyes.
Sparrows' covert conversations, weave of goldfinches
in the undulating shuttle of the wind,
tap, tap, tap of hollow stalks.
Elms scatter gold like profligate kings;
misty wedge of gossamer moon.
The morning sky brims with promise.

TO GARDEN

is to compromise,
accept that while the law allows

division of the land,
life is only leased

from the arbiters of soil;
you will be Sovereign

of your portion, ruled
by the vagaries of seasons,

boundaries transgressed at will
by foxes, pests, diseases, ingress

of vagrant seeds and creeping roots.
Understand that what you grow

is seen as open table:
badgers in the sweetcorn,

insidious slug and snail,
wasps deep inside the apple.

Burden yourself with patience
to allow a second chance

for the squash to plump in Autumn's rain,
laggard parsnips to mature. You are subject

to Adam's curse so must
give more than you receive,

remember, above all else,
that what you harvest is a gift
for your service to the land.

SALTINGS

Here nothing grows tall or large except the sky
stretched above this unflamboyant ground.

Vast, veined cortex, sea-washed, filled and drained,
negotiable land where wind and soil and water
work off each other in fluent stasis.

Salt tongues follow the pendulum of the moon
to bring their words twice-daily,
fill the creeks and channels; mercury-pulse,
whispers of assertion and withdrawal, gentle,
like the quiet telling of a story.

This is a place of modest colours: winter's
grey-lag geese among the sea-brite's orange tips,
prairie sagewort's silver-grey,
perennial curlew prospecting slick, mud banks
for tidal gifts.
Restrained blue and pink of lavender and thrift.

This is a place for other lives,
where we can walk, wary of quags and brackish
pools,
not with the redshank's careful tread
across voracious mud but on blue-baked clay.

We leave no footprint, merely a trace of our passing
through.

Boats are moored; optimistic plans
to find the open sea; others rust and rot
like discredited creeds and dogmas.

This is a place to come for silence
but welcome the wind and the oyster-catchers
piping;
to open out as you walk
towards the sea, pause and return replete;
where tranquillity takes root and finds at least
a margin, perhaps a place more central,
a stab of joy in what you'd overlooked before,
a hope you could return and find again
a state of temporary grace.

This is a place where I lose and find myself.

CUMBRIAN WAY 2016

The valleys' route;
half-way north from Ulverston;
so many opportunities missed,
Coniston Old Man, the Langdale Peaks,
another life-time needed and yet,
each day filled with anything but regret.

A ROAD OF THORNS

SEA HOLLY

Purple-ruffed
silver-grey ladder of nails
rises from the shingle
to stab the incautious hand
of the curious child
or mariner tossed out of the waves,
grasping in the dark
for something tangible,
cursing the wounds which signal rescue.

THE WAR AGAINST SPEECH

Plosives, constantly percussive
are stripping the woodlands of its words
and lacerating speech.
d-d-d-d-d-d-d
a woodpecker pauses,
abandons its siege of bark and sap.

Splintered tongues falter on first syllables,
-hildren –hildren -ood –ater - ater.
Burning, the bones of abbreviated vowels
sear the forest floor; smoke rises, chokes birdsong;
speech flails in labials and fricatives.

A mother croaks a fevered lullaby
in the catacombs of night.
A murmuration of terminal breaths swirls languidly
downwards to roost on cellar floors
and rustle along the silent subway's rails.

Libera nos, libera nos, libera nos;
a train heaves in 4/4 time
huddled shapes of desperation;
suppressed groans over untreated wounds
leaking pus of sibilance and gangrene.

Carefully targeted, relentless, percussive.
Their voices are the drums

their voices are the guns
their voices are the hammers
beating words deep into the soil,
deeper into the granite strata.
The hammer on the anvil
the hammer on the anvil.

Word hoards shrink to mumbled pleas,
to questions of survival
and the last true voices
are the screams of children
rising above the voices of the guns,
articulating terror.

FLIGHT

Gone   the final draughts of golden wine

from this last edge of cliff
            it is time
                to soar beyond the manacles of
land.

her arms un-pinion proudly;
      albino plumage extends and tenses
                       primed
for the moment
      to plot her sidereal path southwards

                to the oceans   un-
tempered.

FIRE-RAISING

Start with the fires,
                allotment sheds,
                        four until they caught him.

Start in his blank-walled room
                with shrugs and mumbled words
                        eyes staring at the floor.

Start with the sheds he chose, a history of
verbal maulings,
                knuckled blows,
                        the estate's small wars, its local
justice.

Start elsewhere
        with the fragments of each day
            the tepid, vacant hours,
                the not being "there"
                    or not wanted anywhere

and follow where that grows day by day
                as deep-chambered magma
                        and the flare of incandescence
                            a boy on the edge of the map
until that moment.

Start with what might grow
    from that blackened husk
        haloed by fire
           in a green place, fed by streams.

WINTER BLEAK

Fire spark and sputter in the pit of winter,
in the deep nocturnal terminus
between harvesting and sowing.
Each day, hunt in the fields and woods,
until the time to slaughter a beast,
feast and fill the moon-flecked hours
with ale and mead, open up
the story hoard, the epic journeys
of gods and heroes, warriors and mythic beasts;
bowls of words spiced, refilled,
passed from lip to ear, carried outside
to catch the dancing of the stars.

Then the crabbed months of counting stores,
eking out on longer nights
the small essential change
of what grew well or failed,
the seasons' mutability, burials and births,
the enduring sub-text
of fear and aspiration. Until longer nights
when speech is locked in frozen ponds
and a sort of sleep, alert for the dog's alarm,
the musky scent of wolves.

AMONG THE WAVES

Our beach!
We had made that claim many years before
in the brimming days of new-found love
and sealed our pledge with hearts
inscribed on the pages of the sand. No witnesses
save the listening sea and ozone-heady gulls.

We came back every year with growing family
and friends, exploring all the rock-pools for starfish,
crabs, bladderwrack and kelp, thrilled
to share our theatre of tumbling cliffs and foam.

Years later, on our own and grateful for the new-
built steps
we'd walked past flies waltzing around a sheep's
bloated corpse, cried against discarded nets,
plastic flotsam, nylon cordage
where moats had once been dug and castles built.

Now, constrained by lockdown and spring-time
storms,
struggling to uphold the framework of each day
against his mind's daily,slow retreat:
? ????   ??   ?????!
I waited, fretted by tightening cords
until I could plan a return. I would

take my husband's hand and talk, reminder on
reminder,
how we had gone before dawn, stumbled down
the stony track to sit in the night's profundity
until the light breached the skin of the sky,
and its heat filled our naked flesh.

Now we stand above the broken steps
and the landslip spreads to the waters' edge,
the torn, dishevelled fencing. I turn
and try to read his face, his moistening eyes:
let him lean into my breast, hear again
his futile plea.

Into the ear of the wind
I whisper a plea for mercy,
for release.

DRY

the river runs at source
a bed of burning stones

cold,
the long hill of summer
awaiting winter's dark

black,
where rivers run
with licensed sludge.

Fingers pick at dust
in empty purses

the forest breaks
the city falls

falls into a pit
onto bones sucked dry of marrow

and the ghosts of those about to die
scrawl their children's epitaphs
in sand.

THE SWAN IN THE HAWTHORN

Placid Thames, mayflies hatching, breeze, until
the bellowing cracked the air, like a calf abandoned
or a child worn out beyond exhaustion.

At the river's edge, through long plumes
of grass and nettle, a swan trapped between
hawthorn and water, voluptuous neck

bent low in a rage of terror, pure plumage
snagged and no way back. Misadventure
or the back-wash of a too-fast boat

a question I turned in my impotence, swan
and myself victim and spectator, no redress at hand.
The tree had shed its blossom, sprung its thorns.

I watched as the pinioned bird thrashed and ranted,
gathered its force, using its wings as bludgeons,
blow after blow, chord after strident chord, broke
free.

My swan regained the river. Relief released me
from yet another moment when hope and life
died at the feet of impersonal power.

BOUND

They follow the threads of morning's light
to mourn the living, carry the double-weight
of loss. There are no obsequies or rituals,
only the daily acts of love and obligation.
Cordage tightens, sinews weaken.

Words cannot be forged to cut
these ties or coined to purchase salve.
Sunset and dawn, sunset and dawn the black ribbons
unspool, unspool and coil around them.
There is no measure for this double-binding.

POEMS FROM IRELAND

SLACK WATER

saline shift at equipoise
intensity compressed
gathering
like

a climber at the summit
or the base

tears on the edge
of grief

mother at the moment
of birth

deep inhalation
before words of love

inexhaustible
the mass of water
poised

FLAXFORT STRAND

Grandsons' voices counter-point
the oyster-catchers' piping;
a curlew's fluting threads the edge of trees
mirrored in the residue of tide. Slowly,

the fingers of the ocean
work into the channels,
lay argent sheets across the sand,
satin ripples into bands like rings of Saturn.

Footsteps crackle over shell-strewn ground,
soft voices carry from the road,
sky and light and water sing together.

LEAVING SLEA HEAD 1845

When I climbed inside your eyeball
and tunnelled through your brain,
I discovered nothing more
than granite and contempt.

Tomorrow we leave this rotting land,
our blighted home, six babies in the cillineach*
dug in our own backyard.
Their eyes scarcely felt the light,
their mouths the flow of milk.

If we stay we'll be like convicts,
waiting to be hoisted to the noose and fed on air,
then thrown like carrion to the dogs,
our scattered bones our epitaph.

Our starvation is your friend,
our corpses just a rounding error
in the accounts of your estate.

cillineach is an Irish burial ground for un-baptised
infants.

CODA

LASTING POWERS

You start with absolute power if not quite
the right amount or depth of crucial knowledge:
the interpretation of sounds and cries;
or the constant energy levels of the sun at 2 a.m.
on a wintry night when your mind's
like clotted cream sliding off a scone
when you're hoping there's at least one clean nappy,
that you've sterilised the feeding bottle.

And that's the start of the odyssey,
emperor shedding clothes year on year,
reverting more and more to subterfuge
to keep some kind of order when the kitchen bristles
with swords and halberds, pikes and claymores
until the Red Cross can come, open a corridor of
retreat
to some new version of sanity and shelter.

And now, years on, you're discussing the granting
of plenipotentiary powers in case, in case
you lose your grip on the greasy chain
which is keeping your heads above the water -
god knows why you don't let go when it's so bloody
cold -
but you hope that dolphins will bear you away
to a hot beach, to emerge from the shallows,
stroll to a cool shack, sit and savour coconut milk,

FRANK MCMAHON

fish and chicken grilled, let the juice
of mango and papaya ooze down your chin;
and as night falls, tune in to the songs of a strolling band,
the words of a poet trying out new lines.
Next day the dolphins bring family and friends.

So still you hold to this tiny span of time,
fill it with friendship, work and dreams,
memories of a warm beach and a huge sky,
observe the circling sharks, your sins,
all those things you got wrong or never did
and hope, despite all that, your children
saw you exert your powers with care
and sometimes, even, wisely.

IN THE AIR

I find profundities,
birds, moths, trees which double
with the footprint of their shadows,
the ocean's shifting imprint,
protective shield around the globe.

This is the wonder of nights,
constellations, the vast improbability
of origins, wolf's tail, mosquito's wings.

And these are the lowest of days,
air, rivers, earth fouled
by the ravenous ghosts
we breed within our nests.

And this could be the quiet ecstasy of evenings,
the fatigue after work of mitigation,
the nurture of inheritance.

MORNING FIRE

Breath steams as I wait,
impatient, for the walk to begin;
I edge towards a meagre stripe of light,
pray for warmth.

                              Iridescent blur
                         locks onto a branch
                              perpends
                              dives rises
                             prey in beak
                              ingests
                         feathers disrobe
                          their liquid cape
                         settles invigilates
                         the rattling stream.

Elemental bird;
                    I want to stay
                              as plumage ignites sun
and sky.

FIELD TRIP OF THE DAMSEL-FLY

Coincidence   to be here   when the magician opens
                the folds   of her cloak   of water
            sparks of electric blue   rise   rise   rise
         hushed   rustle of sedge   studded
with drying wings
      blue   blue   sparks
electric darts
                    damsel-flies   damsel-flies
    here   there
                    around us
         electric   blue   blue   blue
sparks sip
                    from the draughts of warmth
and light
                ascend   paint the slab-grey clouds
                shimmer   in aerial conjunctions
                charge the air with double wonder

    the children   silent
rapt

                    whispers harvest
                    what we leave behind.

THE BOOK OF LEAVES

It starts with the field where they met.
It was in fact a street or a look across
several tables. In truth I am not sure.
But a field - with shimmer of autumn dew,
silver nets of spiders' webs -
is a fertile place, an open space of possibilities,
for conversations among the songs of variable
winds;
pauses to study, in the light of the probing sun,
other fields, woods, copses, grazing horses;
pauses to absorb what was said and heard. And not.

It continues, a field to pitch a tent,
to settle homes, build family; make room for graves
and the trees at the edge a tableau of grief.
Each year clematis, honeysuckle push towards
the invitation of the sun, infoliate,
spread and inter-twine, wear badges
of seductive flower and fruit.

And always the persistent holly, smooth, firm stem,
ever-dark-green foliage a gloss of burnished leather;
a patient reservoir of sap, spiked with loss
and conflict, blood-red berries tuned to the news
of war and famine yet the green fuse of Spring
hunkers within their crimson globes. It continues:

until the leaves drop, drop and mingle

with the gifts of Autumn's winds,
mille feuilles piling and enfolding.
The field receives, waits out the tides of leaves,

their work of scatter and conversion until snowdrops
assert their counter-claim, daffodil and celandine.

ash   and oak
  elder   and chestnut
sycamore
and ivy

                     comfrey
willow

                                   hornbeam

beech

columbine

and bramble

willow   herb

verbena

acer   maple

rose

and liquidambar..
The field prepares another page.

TREE OF SONG AND BLOSSOM
(i.m. Tony Bennett)

"Because of you…"
Almost to the end
you were singing
for song was you
and you were song,
your gift, your pleasure
to gather us around

your voice, a tree of endless blossom,
roots deep in the dark and bright of us.
Weathered by every season.
your voice was life distilled.
Whichever spring gave rise to song
the note was always pure.

This tree is where we met
and joined our lives within the rings of music.

We place our wreaths beneath the blossoms,
re-tell our life within the songs
which brought us love.

THE MUSEUM OF SILENCES

This building where heavy chains were cast,
now restored, repurposed. Galleries, bare
walls and empty tables wait for people
to bring and share their silences.

Silences, when a fragment of the world
arrested them, a wave flared through their core,
numbed sounds on the edge of their tongue.

A silent rill runs through every room, out
into small courtyard gardens, spaces
for silent release from unbearable
compression or to join the high flight of swifts,
each moment registered like a code on cooling
metal.

Midnight 'phone call,
weight of air thumps against the heart.

Early winter evening, an echelon
of cranes migrating south.

This place awaits your silence.

READING DATES 2024

April 17
2pm, Cirencester Rugby Club; Book Launch

April 26
1pm, Poetry Cafe, Cheltenham

June 10
2pm, Cirencester Library (Writers in the Library)

May 1
7pm, online Crafty Crows, Gloucestershire Poetry Society

September 8
6pm, Buzzwords, Exmouth Arms, Cheltenham

ACKNOWLEDGEMENT

Several poems have appeared in Sarasvati, (Indigo Dreams), Acumen, The Cannon's Mouth, "Can you hear the people Sing?" anthology (Palewell Press) and Wildfire Words.

"Saltings" first appeared in the anthology The Wild Night Sky and is reproduced with the kind permission of Crumps Barn Studio, Cirencester.

"The War against Speech" won the Gloucestershire Writers Network Prize in 2022 and was printed in their "Voices" anthology.

I also want to place on record my deep appreciation to my fellow writers in The Somewhere Else Writers and Wordbrew groups.

Also for the wonderful support from Juliette Morton (Dialect Writers), Anna Saunders (Cheltenham Poetry Festival) and Josephine Lay (Gloucestershire Poetry Society).

ALSO FROM TIM SAUNDERS PUBLICATIONS

Hong Kong by Mary Levycky
The Price of Reputation by Lin Bird
A Lesson in Murder by Lin Bird
Love and Death by Iain Curr
The Fourth Rising Trilogy by Tom Beardsell
Letters from Chapel Farm by Mary Buchan
That was now, this is then
by Philip Dawson-Hammond
Healthcare Heroes by Dr Mark Rickenbach
Shadows and Daisies by Sharon Webster
Lomax at War by Dan Boylan
A Life Worth Living by Mary Cochrane
Faze by MJ White
A Dream of Destiny by DoLoraVi
Dreams Can Come True by Rebecca Mansell
The Collected Works of TA Saunders

tsaunderspubs.weebly.com

Unsolicited manuscripts welcome

Printed in Poland
by Amazon Fulfillment
Poland Sp. z o.o., Wrocław